APES

Sandie Lee Books

Apes

The ape species is not a monkey - monkeys have tails and apes do not. Apes are in the Hominidae family. This includes orangutans, chimpanzees, gibbons, gorillas and humans. Apes are very intelligent and very social. Ape fossils have been found in Asia, Europe and African. These fossils suggest the ape may have been around for millions of years. Let's explore the world of the ape to see what other cool and fascinating facts we can find.

Where in the World?

Did you know the ape species can be found in different parts of the world? The gibbon and orangutan can be found in Asia. The gorilla and chimpanzee are found in Africa. All of these animals like forest regions with lots of trees. Some live in low mountain regions, as well as the rainforest.

The Body of an Ape

Did you know apes vary in size, but they are all quite big? Depending on the species, apes can weigh up to 400 pounds. Apes have fur covering most of their bodies, except for their fingers, palms, face and the bottom of their feet. Their arms are twice as long as their back legs. They have pronounced foreheads and small, front facing eyes and flat noses.

What an Ape Eats

Did you know apes are omnivores? This means they will eat both meat and vegetation. Gorillas eat mostly vegetation, like plants and shoots. Chimpanzees will dine on termites, fruit, nuts and even small animals. They also like mushrooms and some species of flowers. Apes can spend most of their time eating.

The Ape's Special Ability

Did you know the ape can use sticks as a tool? The ape species is very smart and can even problem solve. Apes have been known to use sticks to poke into termite or ant nests to get them out. Rocks have been used by apes as weapons and also to break open tough nuts.

Apes and Grooming

Did you know apes groom each other? An ape will use its hands and fingers to groom another ape with. This animal will sit and separate the hair of another ape. It will then pick out any parasites, dead skin or debris. The ape uses grooming as a social greeting. Often they will offer to groom another to also defuse a fight.

The Ape's Defense

Did you know apes are very strong? The sheer size and weight of an ape is enough to put up a fight with another animal. Apes also use their sharp and powerful canine teeth to bite and to wound another animal. These animals have also been known to throw rocks and other objects in a fight.

The Ape as Prey

Did you know the ape is hunted by man? The gorilla has been hunted by man for its hands. These are made into ashtrays. Apes are also hunted for their meat. This is called, bushmeat. Large jungle cats will also hunt young or very old apes for food. The anaconda snake is also a predator to some of the ape species.

Ape Talk

Did you know apes use sounds to communicate? Apes can hoot, whistle, grunt, howl and make barking sounds. Often an angry ape will slap the ground or other objects. It can also pound on its chest and make facial expressions. Male apes will also scent mark their territories with their urine.

The Ape Mom

Did you know most species of apes carry their young for around 9 months? The mother ape can become pregnant between the ages of 8 to 10, depending on the species. The mother ape will nurse her baby milk, like a human mom. She is very protective of her baby and will let it ride around on her back or clinging to her chest.

The Baby Ape

Did you know the baby ape is helpless when it is a newborn? Baby apes are born with fur on their bodies and their eyes open. It is small and may only weigh around 4 pounds. Baby apes learn from watching the adults in their community. Baby apes are often groomed by other members of the community.

Apes at Rest and Play

Did you know apes like to play? Like us, apes like to engage in play. They will climb and swing from trees, wrestle one another and play games of tag. Baby apes will even tumble and play with their feet. In the wild, apes will sleep in tall trees to stay safe from predators.

Life of an Ape

Did you know apes live in communities? Apes like to be with one another. Young apes may still within their family and community for many years, leaving only to find a mate. Apes can live to be quite old. Depending on the species, some apes can live to be over 50 years of age.

Gorillas

This species of ape can grow to be around 400 pounds for males and 200 pounds for females. They are very stocky and strong animals. The gorilla has a very pronounced forehead and a flat nose. They have black fur. The Silverback gorilla has silver hair on its back when it reaches adulthood.

Orangutans

This animal is found in Asia. It lives in the rain-forest and has bright reddish-orange fur. Males of this species can grow to be around 260 pounds and have an arm span of 6.6 feet. They like to eat bird eggs, shoots, leaves and most importantly, fruit. In fact, fruit is the biggest part of their diet.

Quiz

Question 1: Where doesn't the ape have fur?

Answer 1: Its fingers, palms, face and the bottom of its feet.

Question 2: What does the ape use to poke into a termite's nest?

Answer 2: A long pointy stick

Question 3: What do apes do to defuse a fight?

Answer 3: They will groom one another

Question 4: What will an angry ape do?

Answer 4: Slap the ground and other objects

Question 5: Where do apes sleep to stay safe from predators?

Answer 5: In the trees

Thank you for checking out another addition from Sandie Lee Books! Make sure to check out Amazon.com for many other great titles.

www.ingramcontent.com/pod-product-compliance
Lightning Source LLC
Chambersburg PA
CBHW050800290526
45792CB00008B/2264